W9-ARO-051

WESTMINSTER SCHOOLS

SMYTHE GAMBRELL
LIBRARY

PRESENTED BY

Eric Guthrie

Learning About Dragons

by Birdie Stallman
illustrated by Lydia Halverson

CHILDRENS PRESS, CHICAGO

27388

Library of Congress Cataloging in Publication Data

Stallman, Birdie, 1911-
  Learning about dragons.

  (The Learning about series)
  Includes index.
  Summary: Briefly presents dragon lore from many
countries, as well as other facts and fiction about
this "make-believe" monster."
  1. Dragons—Juvenile literature.   [1. Dragons.
2. Folklore] I. Halverson, Lydia.   II. Title.
III. Series: Learning about series.
GR830.D7S7   398.2′454   81-4746
ISBN 0-516-06531-9   AACR2

Learning About Dragons

Created by

THE CHILD'S WORLD

What do you do with a dragon? Slay it? Run from it?
Feed it warm milk?

That depends on what kind of dragon you dream up.
Dragon-dreaming isn't hard to do. The dragons are
there, in your mind. They're just waiting for you to let
them come out.

The idea of scary monsters is very old. But dragons were the first scary monsters people believed in. Of course, dragons are make-believe monsters. They are only real in stories or on TV.

But don't tell a dragon that!

Parents used to tell their children what dragons looked like.

"A fire-breathing snake with scales all over!" said some.

"A flying crocodile!" said others.

"A man-eating monster with seven heads!"

Can a dragon be all those things?

Yes. Everyone sees something different when he sees a dragon.

Dragons come from all different places in all shapes and sizes. Some of them are even nice.

Some of them.

Where did the first dragon come from? Who made up the very first one?

No one knows. Some people think the first dragon was born to explain the weather—rain and lightning and thunder.

Long ago, people didn't know much about the weather. All of a sudden they would see a flash! Light in the sky! Then darkness. Then CRASH! No wonder they made up dragons.

Other people think dragons are all the animals people fear, put together and made bigger. Dragon shapes and parts come from scary animals. That's why many dragons look like snakes or crocodiles. Their spare parts come from bats or tigers or toads.

Maybe both of these ideas are right. Maybe they are both wrong. What do you think?

Dragons can be very different from each other. The dragons we know best are the big, bad ones. But the Chinese say that some dragons are as small as silkworms—and as helpful!

The way a dragon looks and acts depends on where it lives.

SCARY DRAGONS

In Babylonia—
The First Lady of dragons was

Tiamat

This dragon was too big to measure. She had a scaly snake's body and horns on her head. That's a lot of bad scenery!

Tiamat's children weren't very nice either. Tiamat fought her son Marduk in a long battle. Finally, Marduk sent a flash of lightning to Tiamat's heart. That was the end of the First Lady.

People said Marduk used half of Tiamat's body to make the heavens. He used the other half to make the earth.

That lady was a BIG dragon.

In Egypt—
Every night's the same for

Apep

Apep is a fun name to say. But Apep would not have been fun to meet. Apep looked like a serpent and lived in the dark.

The sun always ran into Apep after a hard day of shining. The dragon hated the sun and tried to kill it.

Luckily, the sun's helper, Seth, was as fierce as the dragon. When Apep attacked, Seth killed the dragon and saved the day.

But this dragon didn't stay dead! Seth had to kill that slimy serpent every night so the sun could rise every morning.

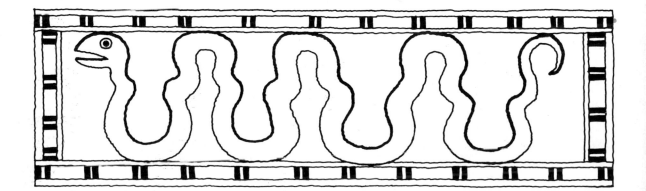

Don't you think they'd get tired of the same old fight?

In Scandinavia—
The people still talk about

Nidhoggr

He was called the "Dread Biter." He hated everything and everybody. With a name like Nidhoggr, you might be unhappy, too!

In his slimy cave, Nidhoggr gnawed and gnawed at the root of the universal tree. He wanted to kill the tree. That would mean the end of the universe.

Every day, workmen repaired the tree. But every night, Nidhoggr gnawed some more. The Norsemen said this gnawing would go on forever.

Maybe they should have changed his name!

In Germany—
It took a trick to get

Fafnir

Once there lived a greedy giant named Fafnir. He cheated his father and brother out of a great treasure.

Then he guarded the treasure so well that he turned into a dragon! That's what happens to greedy giants.

Siegfried, a friend of the family, worked out a way to get the treasure back. He hid in a pit. When Fafnir crawled across the pit, Siegfried pierced the dragon's belly.

It took a trick to kill such a greedy monster.

Before Treasure

After Treasure

Sometimes treasure is bad for your health.

In North America—
The Cherokee Indians fought

The King of the Rattlesnakes

In the mountains of North America there lived a dragon-snake known as the King of the Rattlesnakes. On his head, he wore his most prized jewel—a magical stone.

Naturally, the Cherokees wanted the stone. Wouldn't you?

Many braves died trying to kill the dragon. Nothing worked. Then one warrior made a suit of armor out of leather. Maybe that would protect him from the dragon's fangs!

The brave in leather armor climbed the mountain. The dragon had never seen leather before. The warrior killed the confused dragon. And the Cherokees got the magical stone.

Remember that trick the next time
you go rock hunting.

In England—
There's a day named after

St. George

But George wasn't a dragon.

George was a soldier. He rode through many countries on his horse. One day, he came to a land that was black and bare. George knew a dragon lived there.

The people of the land were very sad. At first they had fed the dragon sheep to keep him happy. But soon the sheep were gone.

Then the dragon had asked for children. And finally, the dragon demanded the King's daughter.

George got very angry. "The princess will live!" he shouted.

Swiftly he rode to the dragon's cave. The monster turned to meet the man.

George pulled his helmet down to cover his face. He speared the dragon again and again. In the end, the mean monster died.

The King offered George much gold and silver. But George didn't want a reward. He had saved the princess.

People don't go into dragon-slaying for the money.

In Ethiopia—
Early to bed wasn't so bad for

The Big Mouth Dragons

These dragons were tricky. They slept with their mouths open! Birds would fly close by. They thought sleeping dragons were safe. But these dragons could eat while they slept.

Too bad, birds!

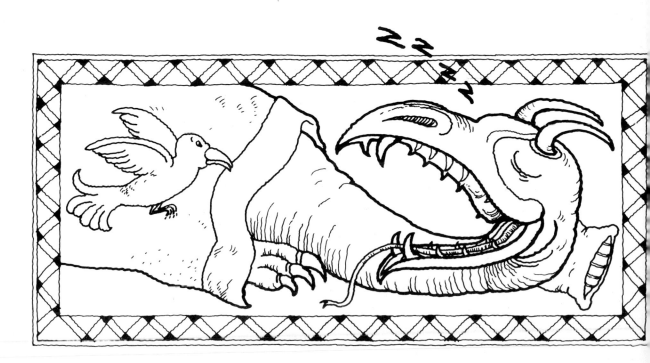

Another trick these dragons knew was boat-making. If one dragon wanted to cross the sea, it just found four or five friends.

Splash! Lash! The dragons would twist their bodies together to make a boat. Heads up, they would sail across the sea.

This probably won't work with your friends.

In Greece—
A pet never forgets, especially

The Baby Dragon

Once upon a time a little boy found a baby dragon. The boy brought the baby home. He loved his new pet and let it sleep by his bed.

But the boy's parents didn't like the dragon at all. One day, the father took the dragon into the desert and left it there.

So much for pet dragons!

The boy grew to be a man. One day, he went on a long journey to a far country. Suddenly, thieves attacked him!

Right away a great dragon appeared. It helped the man fight the thieves. The thieves were no match for the dragon.

What a happy reunion! The dragon was the same one the boy had loved!

It pays to be nice to your pets.

FRIENDLY DRAGONS

Now you know all about scary dragons. You know enough to stay out of their way.

If you lived east of Egypt, you wouldn't have to worry about dragons. Well, not as much anyway.

Eastern dragons have better ways of getting what they want. Like western dragons, they love treasure. But they would rather drink warm milk than eat beautiful maidens.

Western dragons lurk in caves. Eastern dragons live in water. That's the secret of their power. People from the east believed in dragon-gods called Nagas. They thought the rain, rivers, lakes, and oceans were ruled by those dragons.

Eastern dragons could afford to be nice. No one would kill a monster in control of all the water.

In India—
The rain came from

Vritra

Have you ever seen a dragon-shaped cloud?

The Indian people believed in Vritra, dragon of the clouds. They thought Vritra stored rain in its stomach.

So to make it rain, the god Indra shot thunderbolts at Vritra. When he hit the dragon, down came the rain.

That makes a dragon-sized stomach ache!

In China—
Most dragons are like

The Black Dragon

Once a Chinese emperor went to visit the Black Dragon near Peking. At the Black Dragon Pool, he called the mighty monster.

After a while, the emperor saw a black dragon about six inches long swim up to him.

The emperor laughed. "Is this the great Black Dragon? You would be invisible in my goldfish pond!"

The dragon did not answer. He lifted one claw from the water. The claw began to grow. First it overshadowed the pool. Then the temple disappeared. Finally, the dragon's single claw covered the mountaintops.

"Come down, come down," begged the emperor. "You are the greatest of all creatures. All that I have is yours. Only come down!"

And the dragon did.

Dragons are not always what they seem.

In China—
Everybody waits for

The Dragons on Parade

At the Chinese New Year's party, a bamboo dragon winds its way through the streets of every village.

The dragon's head is bright red and blue and gold and green. Its body is covered with cloth. Men hide under the cloth to help the dragon walk. Back and forth the dragon sways!

Children cheer! Maybe the dragon will bring them good luck in the new year.

If not, there's always next year.

In Japan—
Children make

Dragon Kites

When the winds blows, so do the kites! The long-tailed kites look like the dragon that is supposed to live in Japan's Inland Sea.

But when you have a kite in your hand, you don't think about dragons much.

Kites are more fun than dragons anyway.

Or are they?

MODERN DRAGONS

Dragons are born every day. Usually they appear in stories.

The Hobbit's Dragon

Bilbo Baggins, a hobbit, knows about storybook dragons. He met a bad one named Smaug once. Smaug is a good name for a dragon. (At least the writer, J.R.R. Tolkien, thought so!)

Smaug's teeth were swords, his claws spears, and his breath death. But the dragon had a soft spot over his heart.

When Bilbo saw the soft spot, he felt more confident. But then the dragon spouted scorching flames at the hobbit!

The dragon didn't live to the end of the story. But Bilbo had learned his lesson. Never be too confident around a dragon.

But storybook dragons can be nice, too. They can even be rather undragon-like.

The Not-Really-A-Dragon Dragon

Eustace hadn't read any of the right books. He didn't know that greedy people can become dragons themselves.

So, not knowing about dragons, Eustace got into trouble. He took a beautiful bracelet. And you can guess what happened next.

Eustace had done one right thing, though. He had made friends with nice people before his days as a dragon. His friends loved him even after he became a dragon.

All the same, aren't you glad you read the right books? (If you haven't read *The Voyage of the Dawn Treader,* you'd better!)

When you know all about dragons, you may meet one!

The Reluctant Dragon

Once there was a Boy who knew all about dragons. So when a dragon showed up near his town, the Boy knew just what to do.

He visited with the dragon. They talked about poetry, mostly. And they got to be good friends.

The townspeople didn't like the dragon, though. They sent for St. George. They wanted him to fight the dragon.

But the dragon didn't want to fight at all! So it was up to the Boy to work everything out. That's hard when you're dealing with a reluctant dragon!

But, in the end, the Saint, the Boy, and the dragon walked off arm in arm.

This is a good story to read if a dragon ever shows up in your town. (It's told by Kenneth Grahame.)

At least one dragon has been seen in this century. Have you heard of it?

The Real-Life Dragon

There is one real-life animal that looks and acts like a dragon. It is the Komodo dragon. It lives on the island of Komodo, in Indonesia.

The Komodo dragon is a lizard. It can grow to be over six feet long! During the day the Komodo dragon hunts for its food, sometimes even killing deer. At night, it digs a cave and hides in it.

The Komodo dragon is not as scary as some of the make-believe dragons. Still, would you want to meet one?

INDONESIA

Pacific Ocean

KOMODO

IF YOU DO MEET A DRAGON . . .

Slay it. Run from it. Feed it warm milk.
But whatever you do, never ignore a dragon.

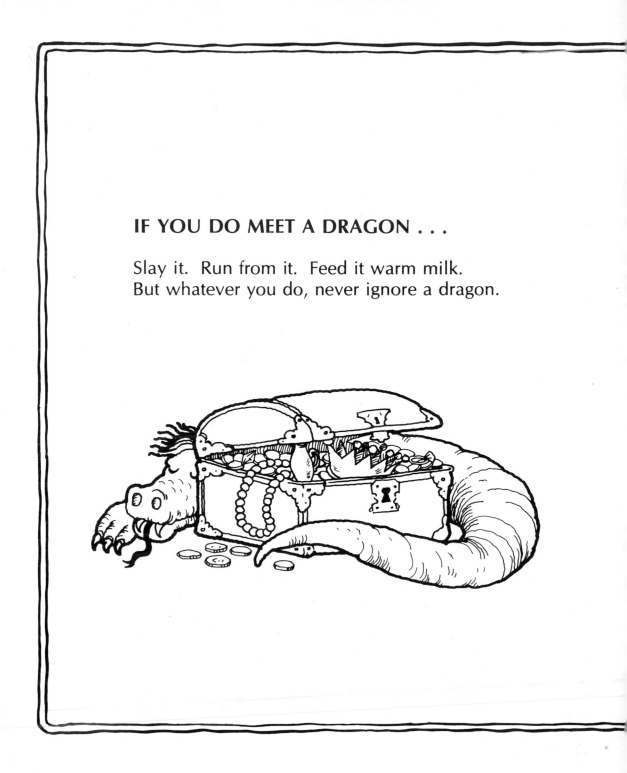

INDEX

Apep, 14-15
Babylonian dragon, 12-13
Baggins, Bilbo, 38
Black Dragon, 32-33
Chinese dragons, 11, 32-35
Egyptian dragon, 14-15
English dragon, 22-23
Ethiopian dragons, 24-25
Eustace, 40-41
Fafnir, 18-19
German dragon, 18-19
Grahame, Kenneth, 43
Greek dragon, 26-27
Indian dragon, 30-31
Indra, 30-31
Japanese dragon, 36-37
Kites, 36-37
Komodo dragon, 44-45
Marduk, 12
Nidhoggr, 16-17
North American dragon, 20-21
Rattlesnake, 20-21
Reluctant Dragon, The, 42-43
St. George, 22-23, 43
Scandinavian dragon, 16-17
Seth, 14-15
Siegfried, 18-19
Smaug, 38-39
Tiamat, 12-13
Tolkien, J. R. R., 38
Voyage of the Dawn Treader, The, 40-41
Vritra, 30-31

3